FEEL BETTER FABLES

MORT
THE
WORRYWART™

Written by Jason Wolf Illustrated by Nathanael Lark

MEANINGFUL MESSAGES MADE SIMPLE™

www.feelbetterfables.com

Feel Better Fables are stories for everyday people, by everyday people. And we believe that every day people can make a difference.™

After reading my fair share of self-improvement books over the years, I discovered recalling many of the messages and lessons from what I read was sometimes just too overwhelming. Maybe there is such a thing as "too much good information?" And let's face it - what good is any information if you can't remember it?

What I could remember were the meaningful stories and fables I read as a child - stories that inspired me and taught me about life. That's when I realized many of life's lessons could be summed up in fewer words than a well-intentioned book with hundreds of pages.

So I took many of those "life lessons" that taught me so much over the years, and turned them into thoughtful, easy to remember stories about the very issues we all face: Grief, crisis, worry, overcoming obstacles, love lost or found, finding peace of mind, etc. That's when "Feel Better Fables" was born: A company that brings you meaningful messages made simple.

Our mission at Feel Better Fables is to inspire you with simple messages to make meaningful life changes. We believe, when we're inspired to think and see things differently, our life can change. And sometimes all it takes is a meaningful message made simple to do just that!

Enjoy your journey,

Jason Wolf
Founder and President

MORT
THE
WORRYWART™

This is the story of a little Caterpillar named Mort, who was a worrywart.

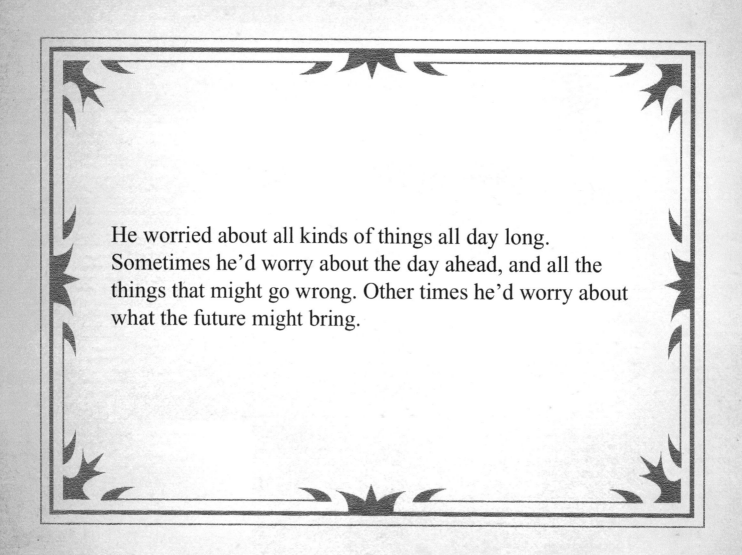

He worried about all kinds of things all day long. Sometimes he'd worry about the day ahead, and all the things that might go wrong. Other times he'd worry about what the future might bring.

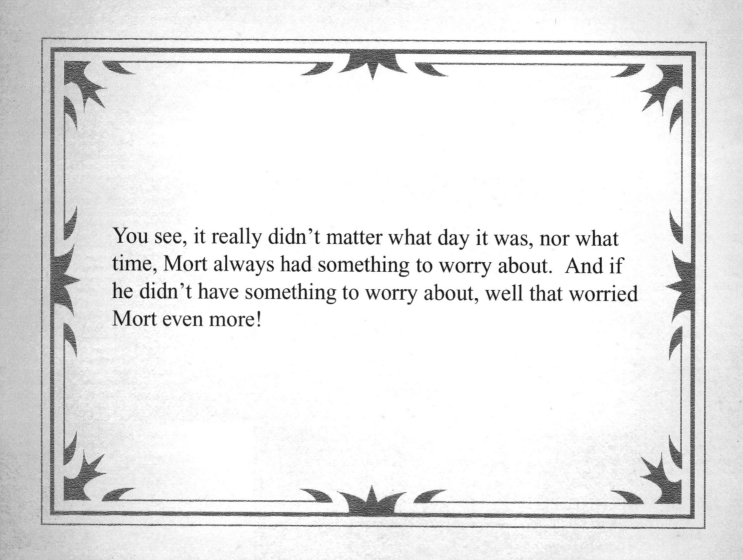

You see, it really didn't matter what day it was, nor what time, Mort always had something to worry about. And if he didn't have something to worry about, well that worried Mort even more!

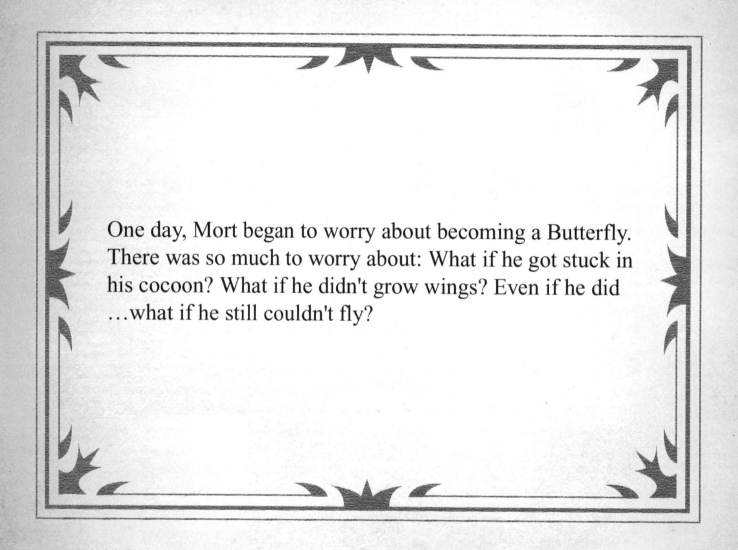

One day, Mort began to worry about becoming a Butterfly.
There was so much to worry about: What if he got stuck in
his cocoon? What if he didn't grow wings? Even if he did
…what if he still couldn't fly?

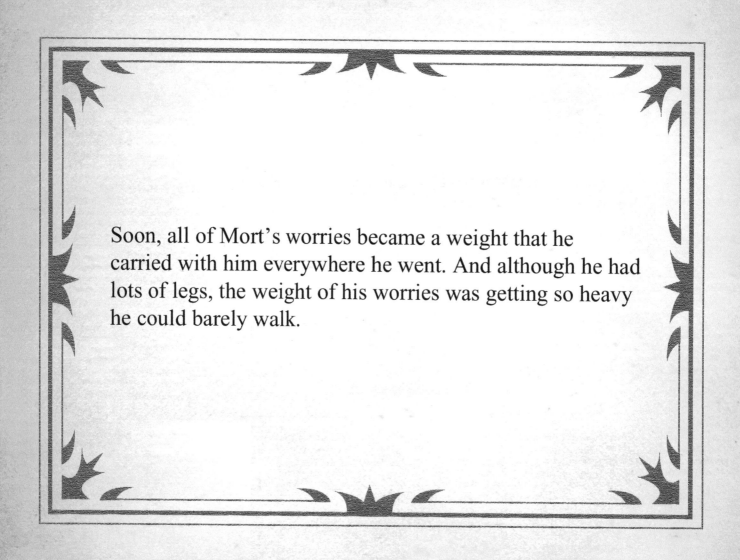

Soon, all of Mort's worries became a weight that he carried with him everywhere he went. And although he had lots of legs, the weight of his worries was getting so heavy he could barely walk.

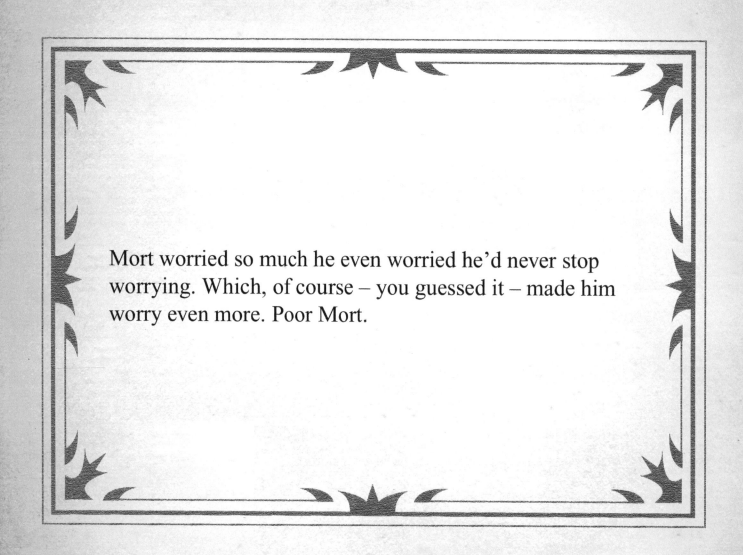

Mort worried so much he even worried he'd never stop worrying. Which, of course – you guessed it – made him worry even more. Poor Mort.

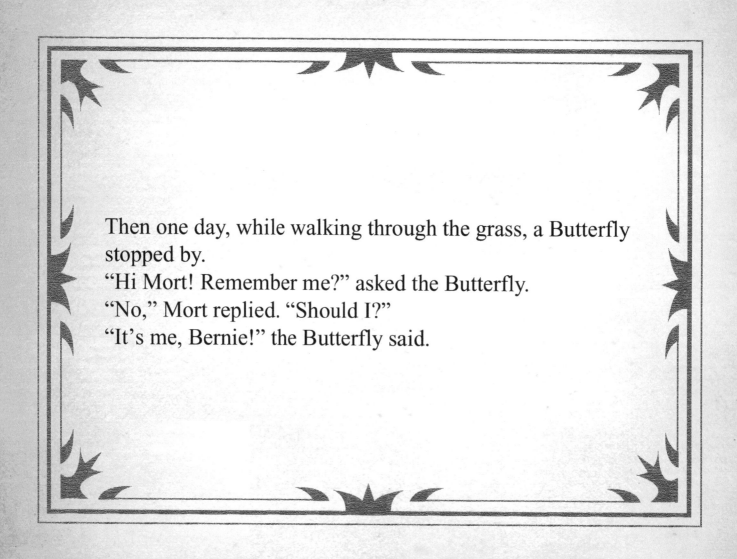

Then one day, while walking through the grass, a Butterfly stopped by.

"Hi Mort! Remember me?" asked the Butterfly.

"No," Mort replied. "Should I?"

"It's me, Bernie!" the Butterfly said.

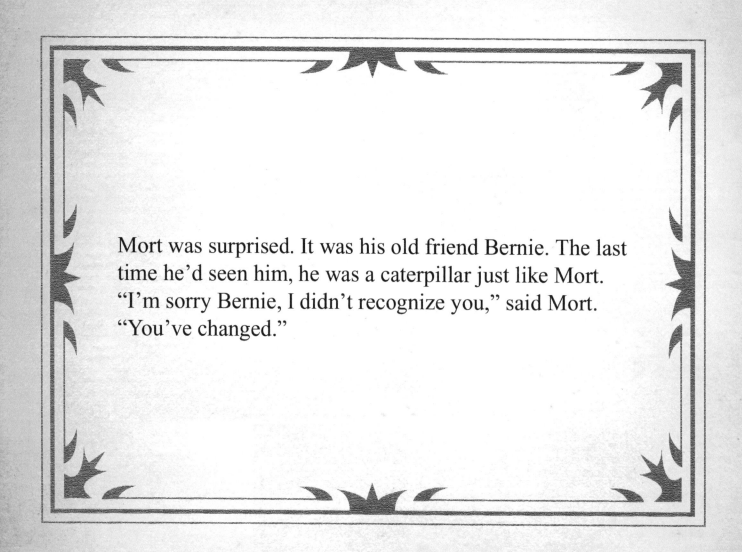

Mort was surprised. It was his old friend Bernie. The last time he'd seen him, he was a caterpillar just like Mort. "I'm sorry Bernie, I didn't recognize you," said Mort. "You've changed."

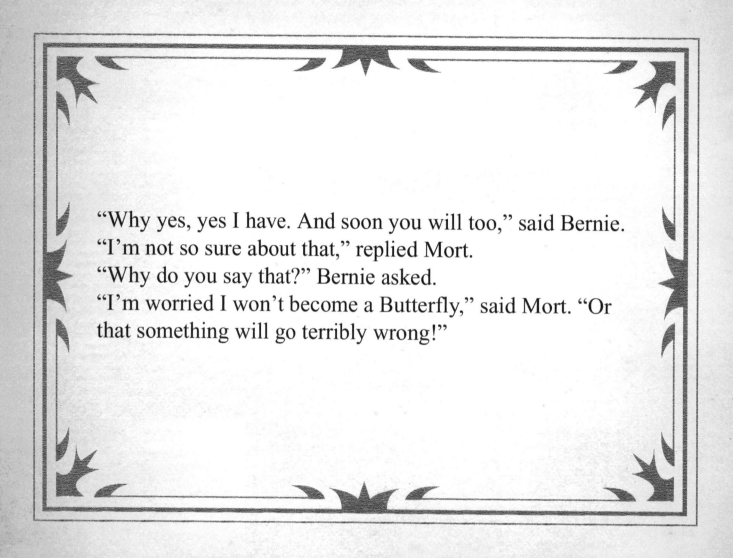

"Why yes, yes I have. And soon you will too," said Bernie.
"I'm not so sure about that," replied Mort.
"Why do you say that?" Bernie asked.
"I'm worried I won't become a Butterfly," said Mort. "Or
that something will go terribly wrong!"

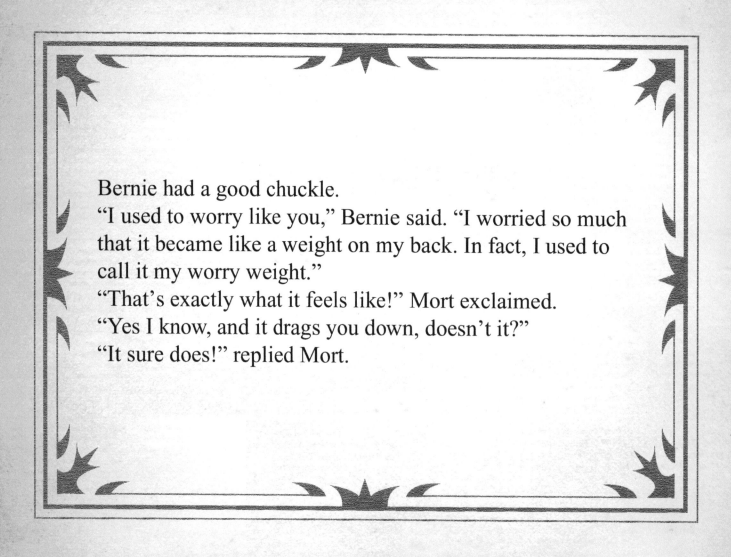

Bernie had a good chuckle.

"I used to worry like you," Bernie said. "I worried so much that it became like a weight on my back. In fact, I used to call it my worry weight."

"That's exactly what it feels like!" Mort exclaimed.

"Yes I know, and it drags you down, doesn't it?"

"It sure does!" replied Mort.

"Luckily, a very wise butterfly told me that when I did become a butterfly it would be very hard to fly if I continued to carry around all that weight. So he taught me how to lose my worry weight by using a simple lesson called the 90% Rule."

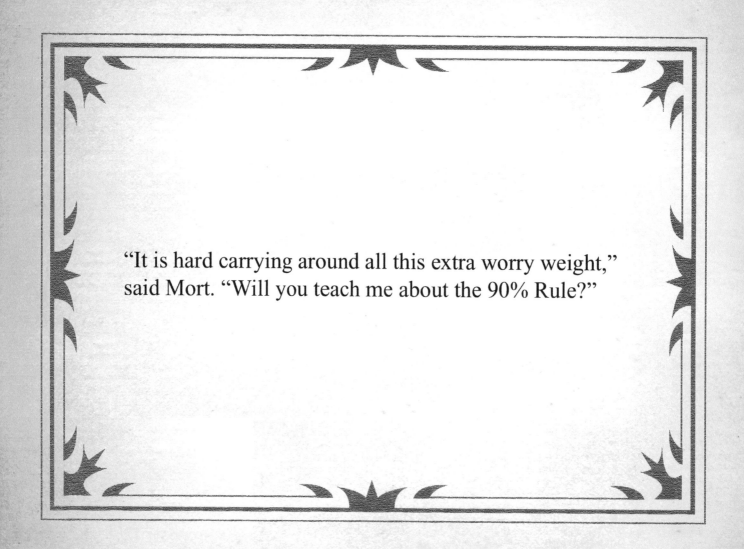

"It is hard carrying around all this extra worry weight,"
said Mort. "Will you teach me about the 90% Rule?"

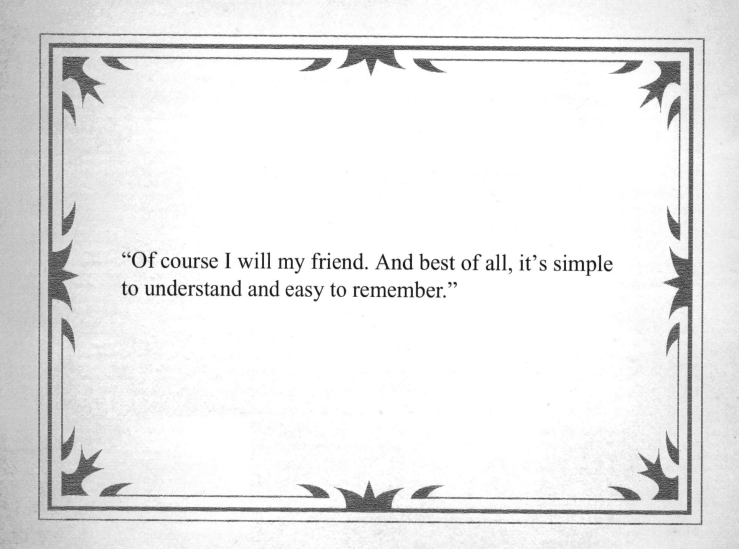

"Of course I will my friend. And best of all, it's simple to understand and easy to remember."

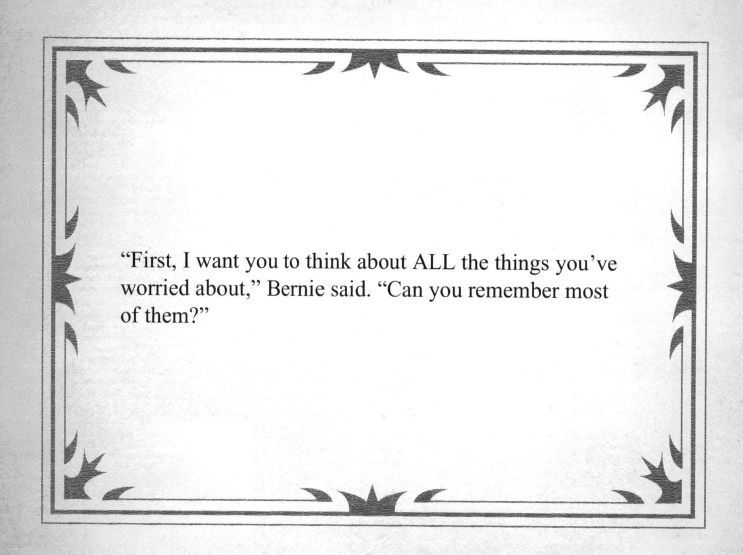

"First, I want you to think about ALL the things you've worried about," Bernie said. "Can you remember most of them?"

Mort thought for a long time and then replied,
"Well no…, actually I can't."

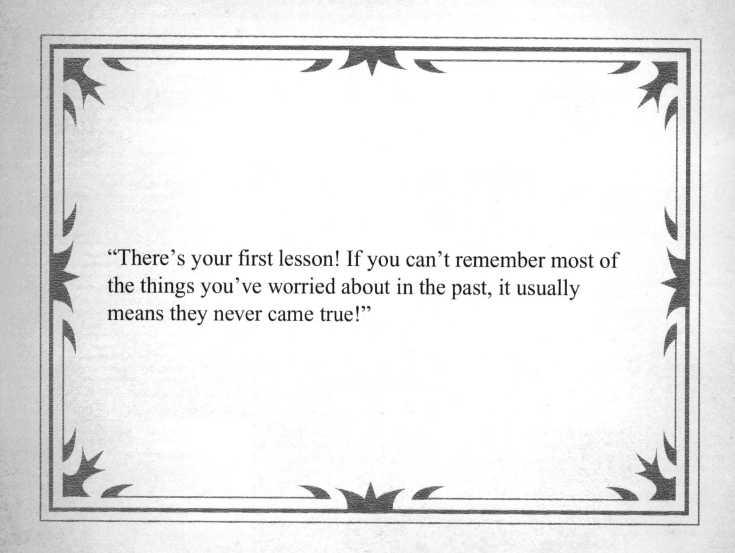

"There's your first lesson! If you can't remember most of the things you've worried about in the past, it usually means they never came true!"

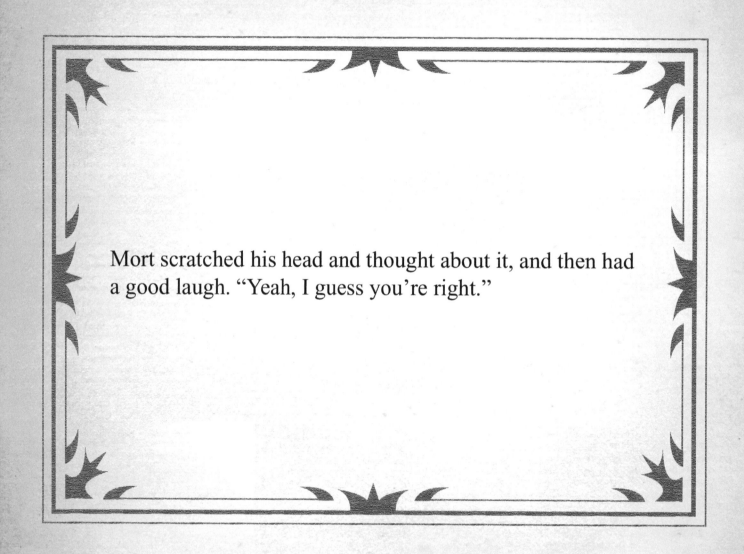

Mort scratched his head and thought about it, and then had a good laugh. "Yeah, I guess you're right."

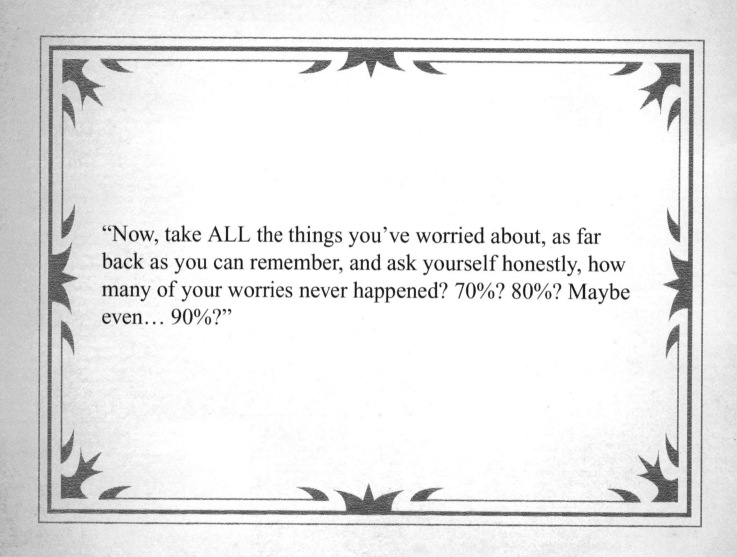

"Now, take ALL the things you've worried about, as far back as you can remember, and ask yourself honestly, how many of your worries never happened? 70%? 80%? Maybe even… 90%?"

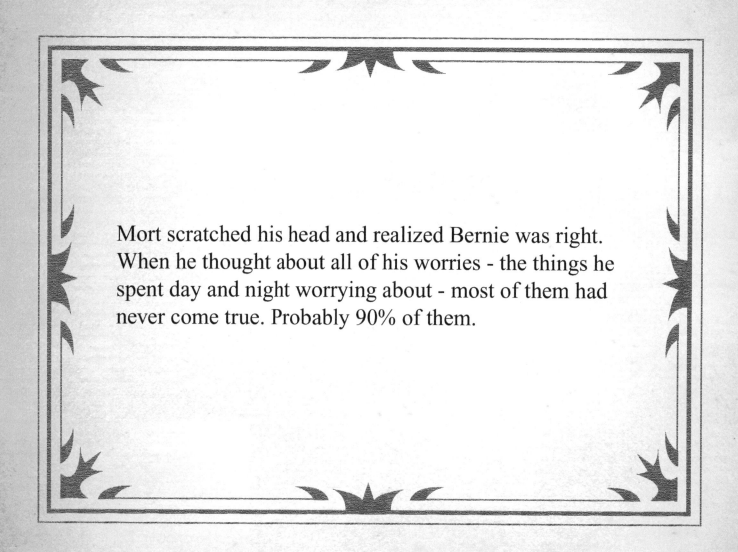

Mort scratched his head and realized Bernie was right. When he thought about all of his worries - the things he spent day and night worrying about - most of them had never come true. Probably 90% of them.

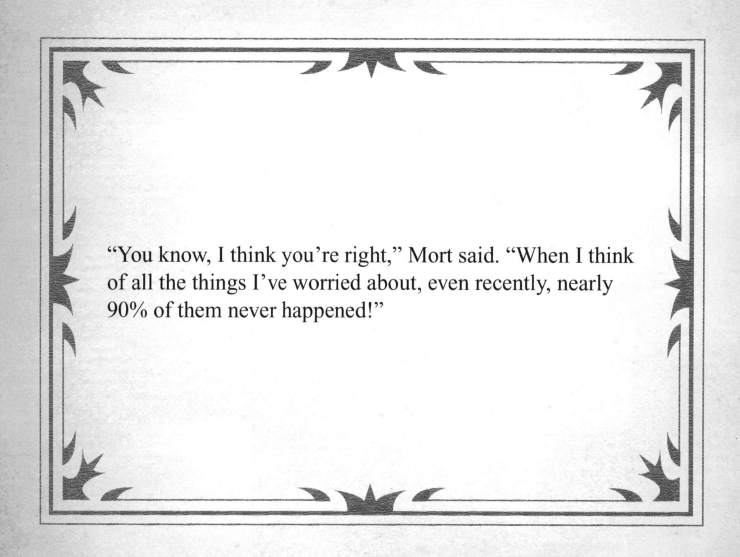

"You know, I think you're right," Mort said. "When I think of all the things I've worried about, even recently, nearly 90% of them never happened!"

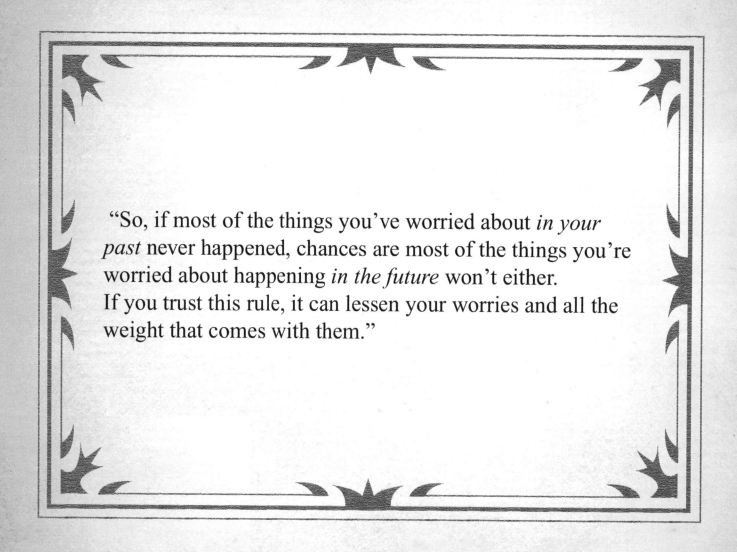

"So, if most of the things you've worried about *in your past* never happened, chances are most of the things you're worried about happening *in the future* won't either.
If you trust this rule, it can lessen your worries and all the weight that comes with them."

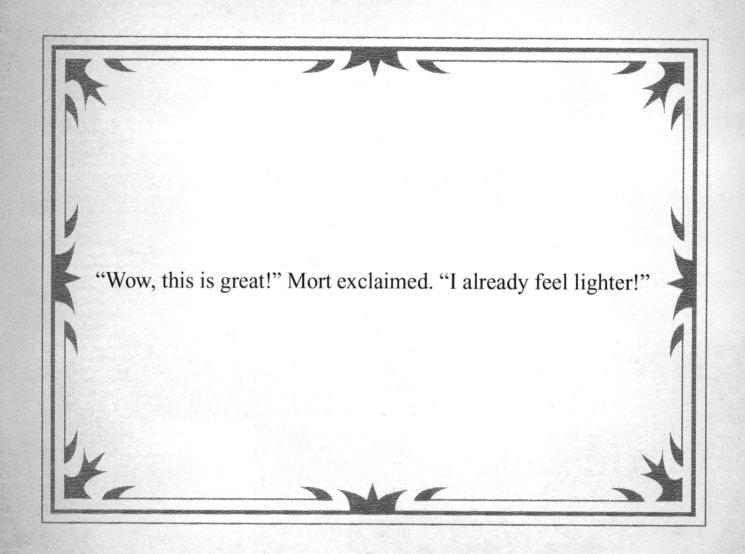

"Wow, this is great!" Mort exclaimed. "I already feel lighter!"

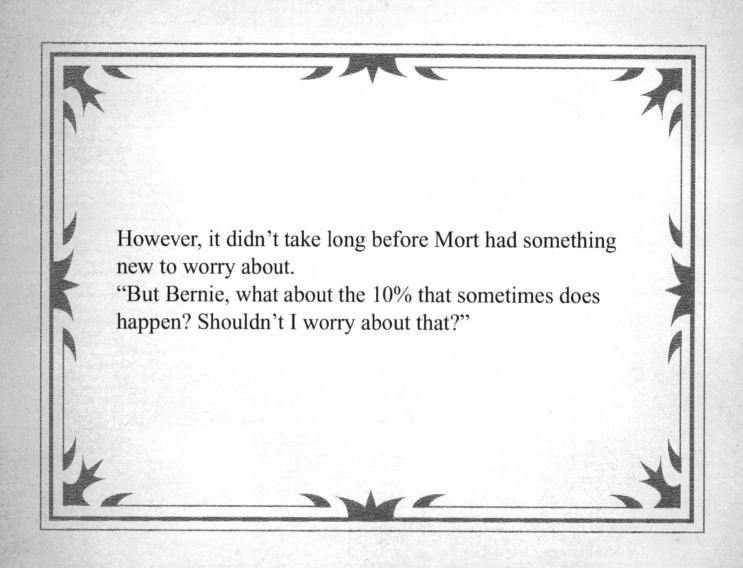

However, it didn't take long before Mort had something new to worry about.

"But Bernie, what about the 10% that sometimes does happen? Shouldn't I worry about that?"

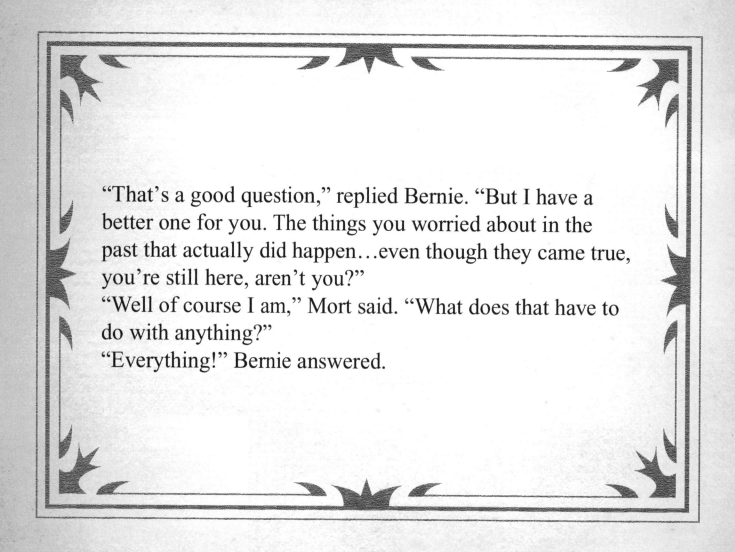

"That's a good question," replied Bernie. "But I have a better one for you. The things you worried about in the past that actually did happen…even though they came true, you're still here, aren't you?"

"Well of course I am," Mort said. "What does that have to do with anything?"

"Everything!" Bernie answered.

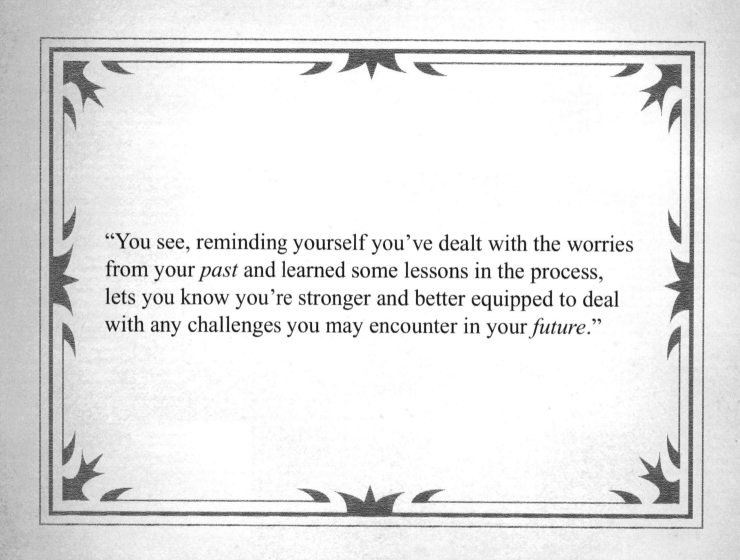

"You see, reminding yourself you've dealt with the worries from your *past* and learned some lessons in the process, lets you know you're stronger and better equipped to deal with any challenges you may encounter in your *future*."

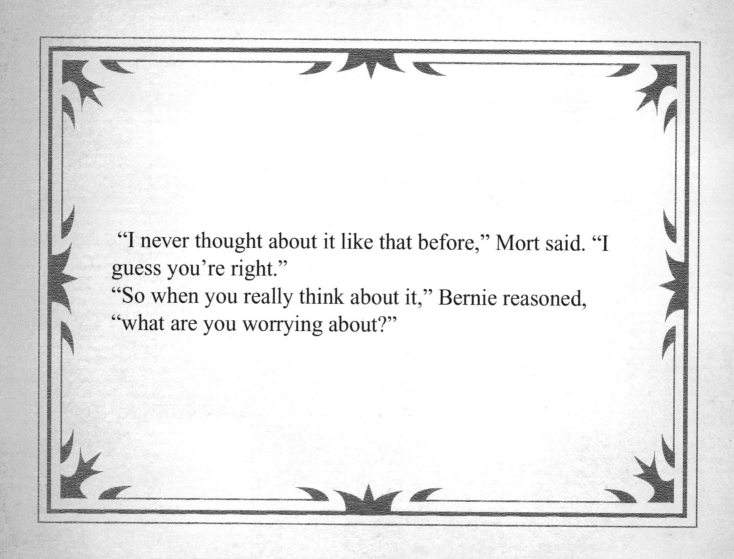

"I never thought about it like that before," Mort said. "I guess you're right."

"So when you really think about it," Bernie reasoned, "what are you worrying about?"

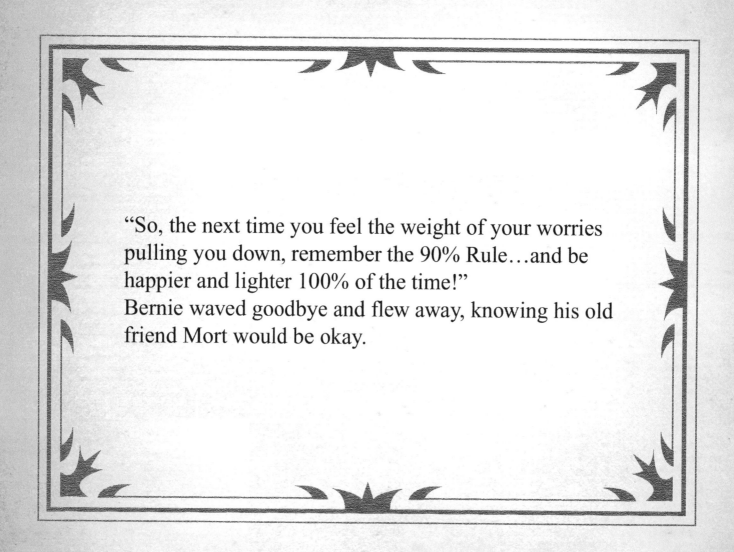

"So, the next time you feel the weight of your worries pulling you down, remember the 90% Rule…and be happier and lighter 100% of the time!"
Bernie waved goodbye and flew away, knowing his old friend Mort would be okay.

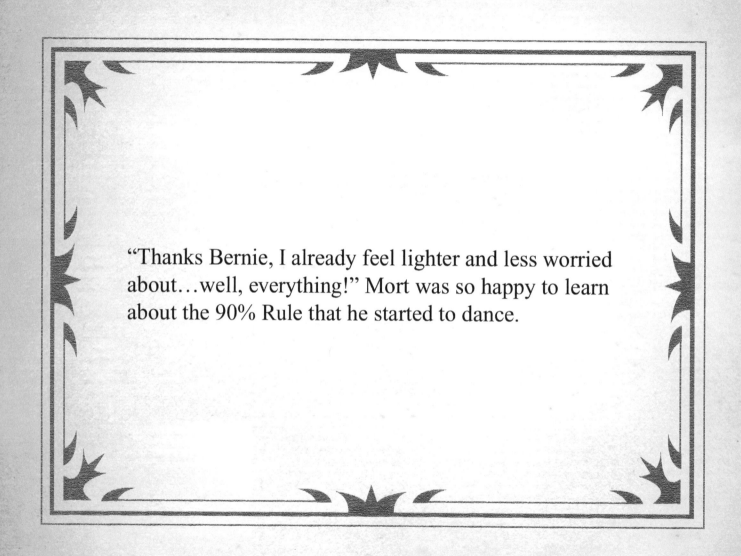

"Thanks Bernie, I already feel lighter and less worried about…well, everything!" Mort was so happy to learn about the 90% Rule that he started to dance.

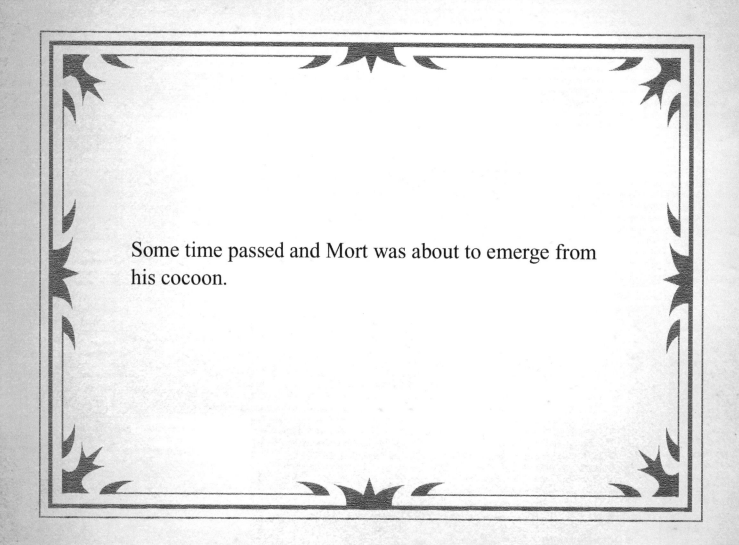

Some time passed and Mort was about to emerge from his cocoon.

Mort was finally a Butterfly – happy and joyful, just like
Bernie said.

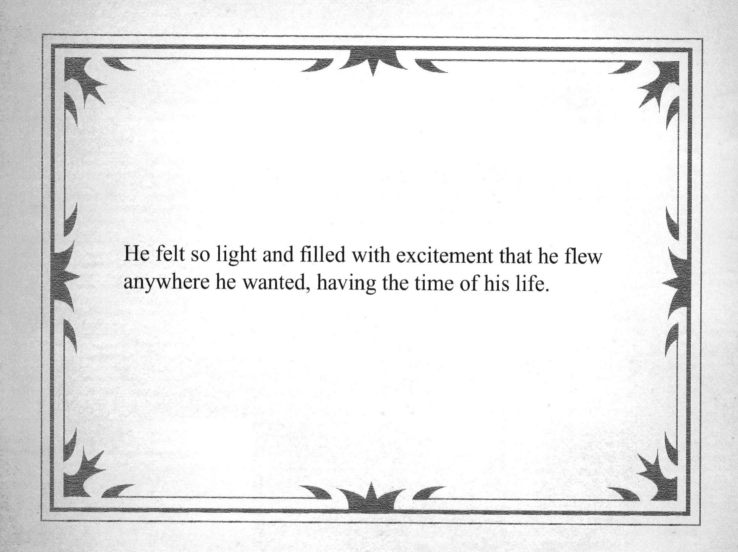

He felt so light and filled with excitement that he flew anywhere he wanted, having the time of his life.

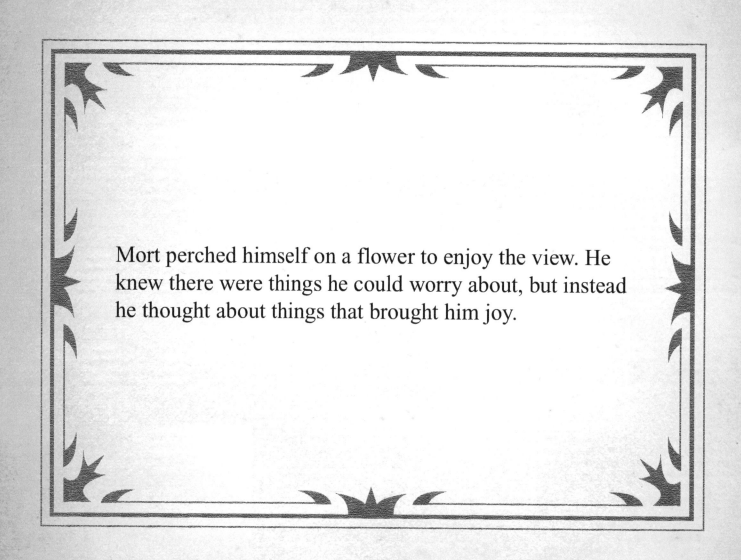

Mort perched himself on a flower to enjoy the view. He knew there were things he could worry about, but instead he thought about things that brought him joy.

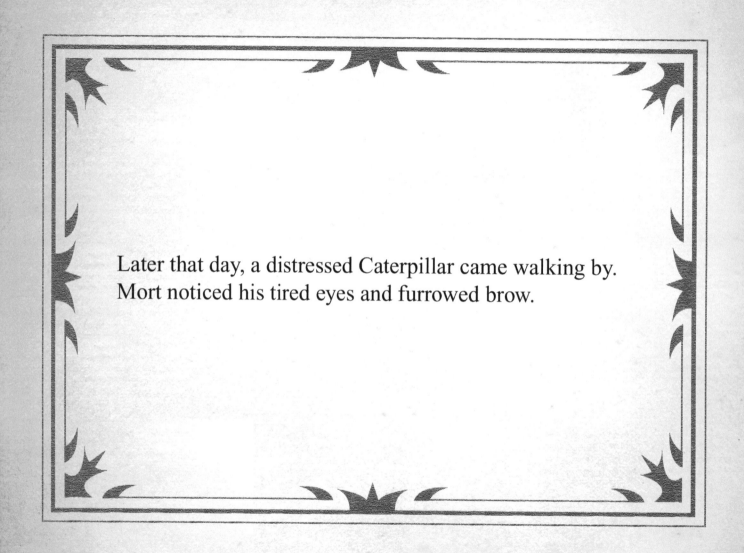

Later that day, a distressed Caterpillar came walking by. Mort noticed his tired eyes and furrowed brow.

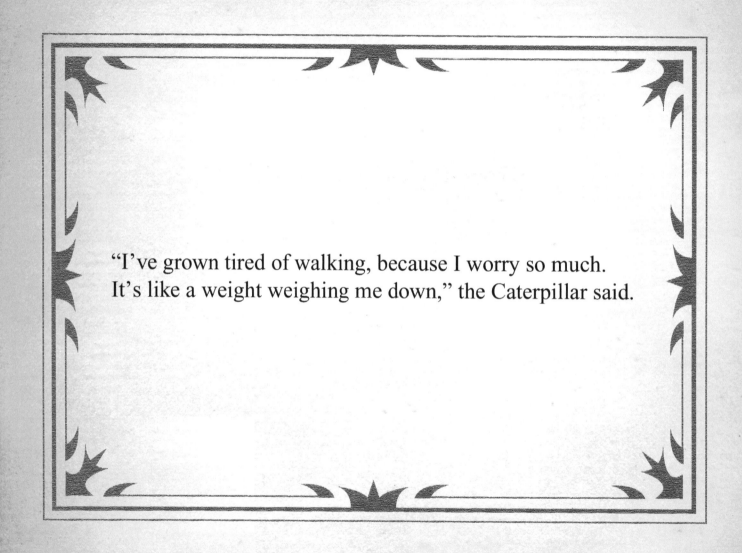

"I've grown tired of walking, because I worry so much.
It's like a weight weighing me down," the Caterpillar said.

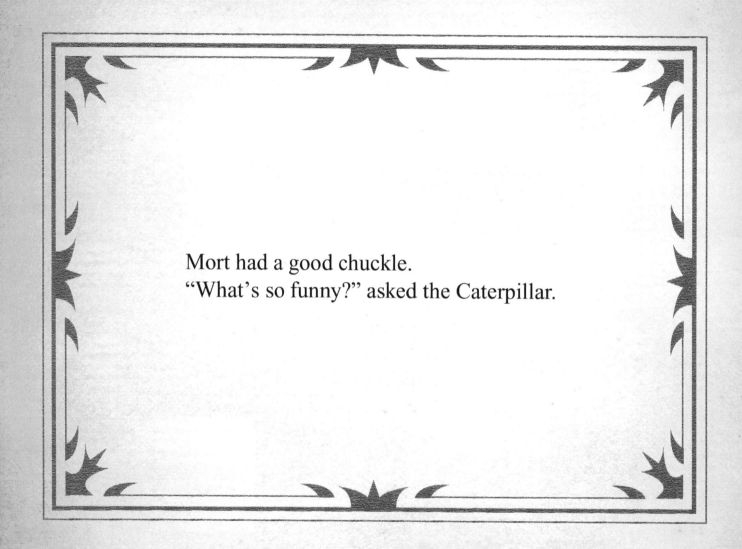

Mort had a good chuckle.
"What's so funny?" asked the Caterpillar.

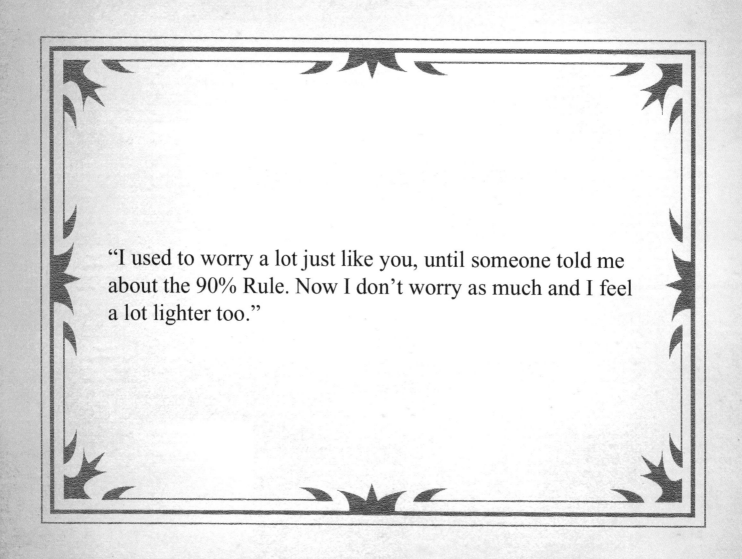

"I used to worry a lot just like you, until someone told me about the 90% Rule. Now I don't worry as much and I feel a lot lighter too."

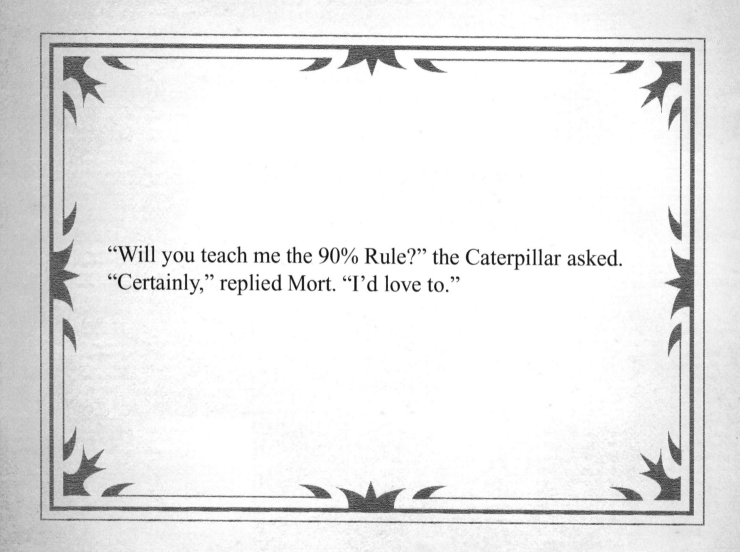

"Will you teach me the 90% Rule?" the Caterpillar asked.
"Certainly," replied Mort. "I'd love to."

The Beginning...

A Meaningful Message to Remember

Who doesn't worry or at least have moments in their life when they do? This human truth is something we all experience - and unfortunately for some people, it happens far too often. With the help of our imagination, we tend to trick ourselves into feeling the stress of what we're worrying about as if we knew for certain it was going to happen - or worse, as if it already has! This can be both mentally and physically exhausting. Yet when we take the time to honestly examine our worries, we're astounded to see that at least 90% - if not more - NEVER happen! We're experiencing these undesirable moments of anxiety, stress and fatigue, along with mental and physical pain, for something that will most likely never happen. If you check in with your own personal experience you'll see how true this is.

Unless we get a grip on our worries, they can easily manifest into sadness, depression, anger and frustration, which ultimately affects our mental wellbeing and our physical health as well. Maintaining a healthy perspective on unnecessary worrying helps you get a grip on it, before it gets a grip on you!

And we get a grip on our worries by realizing worrying is a choice. When we accept this, we immediately empower ourselves with options. For example, to worry, or not worry? Or least, not as much! You see, when we choose not to worry about fearful, disempowering illusions of hypothetical situations that usually never happen, we change the course from an old way of thinking that never served us, brought us joy, or made our life any better. When we choose not to worry - or at least worry less - we empower ourselves to feel better, regain our sense of freedom and enjoy our life again.

When we worry more than we should we are not experiencing something that's "out of our control," but rather we've developed a "habit of thinking." And that habit can be broken. It just takes a little practice. Here are some questions to consider to help you break your pattern:

1. When you stop to consider your worries from as far back as you can remember to present day, how many of your worries NEVER came to be? Is it at least 90%? Or is the percentage maybe even higher? Is it hard to accept that most of your worries won't and don't happen? Maybe it's time to start worrying less. Either way, it's your choice.

2. When you're consumed with worry where do you feel it? In your stomach? Your back? Your chest? Your head? Your breathing? Would you admit these "feelings" are not serving you very well when they arise? How soon after your worries dissolve, or when you discover they won't happen, do these uncomfortable feelings go away? Does it take days, or does it happen soon after? Check in with yourself and ask how your worrying has been serving your day-to-day experience. Maybe it's time to start worrying less. Either way, it's your choice.

3. Do you find it hard to accept the idea that most of the things you're going to worry about tomorrow and into the future won't happen either? If so, why is that? Maybe it's time to start worrying less. Either way, it's your choice.

Look, let's be honest... a little worrying is natural. In fact, at times it can help us reconsider things or inspire us to put a little extra thought into something. But sometimes, enough is enough! So when it comes to worrying, now you have more insight, power and choice in the matter. From now on, for you, worrying is a choice. And when you choose to worry less, you'll be amazed how quickly life becomes lighter and more enjoyable!

At Feel Better Fables we believe you don't have to be a master chef with a degree in the culinary arts to have an incredible recipe for apple pie.

We know many of you have meaningful, inspirational stories that, if shared with others, could make a difference in someone's life. If you have a story that can inspire others about dealing with any of life's challenges, we want to hear it! For more information and our submission guidelines, please contact us at InspireUs@FeelBetterFables.com

Feel Better Fables are stories for everyday people, by everyday people. And we believe that every day people can make a difference.™

MEANINGFUL MESSAGES MADE SIMPLE™

Feel Better Fables

Mort The Worrywart

Enjoy The Ride

How IT found Love, Happiness and Respect

The Island of 72 Degrees

...and many more titles.

More titles available at

www.feelbetterfables.com

About the Author

Jason Wolf is a writer, producer and professional doodler who lives in Los Angeles, California. Feel Better Fables are just one of his many creative endeavors, which include children's books, graphic novels and an inspirational apparel line. As a public speaker and life coach, Jason infuses depth, humor and fun in his approach to helping others see new ways of dealing with age old issues.